White
Tulip

White
Tulip
Ben Thompson

Smokestack Books
1 Lake Terrace, Grewelthorpe, Ripon HG4 3BU
e-mail: info@smokestack-books.co.uk
www.smokestack-books.co.uk

Text copyright 2019,
Ben Thompson,
all rights reserved.

ISBN 9781916012158

Smokestack Books
is represented
by Inpress Ltd

*to the memory of
Geraldine Swingler*

Contents

Part 1 Golden Door Half-Open	9
Part 2 White Tulip	25
White Tulip	27
Solaris	28
Vanishing	29
Lullaby	31
Requiem	33
Inside the Whale	37
Rosemary	41
The Flower Arrangement	42
Litakovo	44
After the Chinese	45
Four Brontë Pictures	46
His Master's Voice	50
Before the Flood	51
The Bells	57
Waves on Water	59
Not in Your Name	62
Soldiers	63
Joanna	66
As for Forever	67
Tables	72
Acknowledgements	73

**Part 1
Golden Door
Half-Open**

1 Bumble Bee

How do they seem,
These horned cousins
That swim on the Earth?

You raise your paw
Like a dancing bear
Defending his circle.

These little cousins
Will pillage your flesh
With infinite care.

2

The evening flows on so slowly
Let us drop some notes into the stream of time,
Let us watch the burnished evening glow
Glide over the strings.

Let us flick notes into space
Like inkblots thrown from a pen,
Call the dancer and his bride who will journey
Through two worlds together.

At the last bar of the last song
The sound briefly echoes in the hollows.
The audience rises in dust
To clap for the sun and the moon.

3

A terrible nightmare befell Slattery
In the ballroom of Owl College.
As he danced in the dark it was his turn to pay for the drinks,
As he felt in his pocket, the lights went up

Revealing him in the cold cowl of dawn
Fingers feeling where the grass had rubber roots,
The smile on his face a 'Gee whiz, fellas'
As his friends faded into the turnip crop.

Now all the world knows Slattery's
In the can with only hell to pay –
His footprints on the faces of the dancers
Gave the game away.

4

This journey so lightly begun
Does not promise a turning back,
Nor do the hooks of farewells
Hold fast.

This crossing into the twilight
Of the heart's heavy zone
With the slow burning of the hours
For fuel

And the fierce pressure of the wind
Stirring the ashes to Eve and back again,
Giving Spring the power to coincide
With the momentary brain.

5

I am a white box
Or bay window traveling
I am your transport

I am the high wing
Of the coal face
A magic fan

A door that opens
On a white landing light
On the sketched in chambers.

6

The field which has just been ploughed
Looks like a frozen sea,
Perhaps it is a frozen sea.

Overhead the wind moves
Tons of water in great sky banks
From one unknowable place to another
For utterly no reason.

Perched on the frozen sea
Yellow birds
Look at me.

7

What is that murmur like a huge ocean?
Only your mind

Said a head
Afloat
In a boat.

8

Small piece of sky in iron hoops,
Frozen wave on a glacier bed

Golden door half open
In sheer cloud walls.

9 Orion

On a clear night I saw
Alnitak, Alnilam, Mintaka
Suddenly stand in their depths,

And all things fused into one.
Then were those great fires
Hanging over me –

And someone on Aldebarran
Was waving to me,
We stood face to face.

10

Corvus perched upon Hydra,
The crow upon the watersnake.

The river of dreams
Is dammed by the earth,

And the lake reflects the fires
Of the fisher on its banks.

11

The stars are anathema to life,
Only through this deep fluid
Can I receive their vibrations.

It shields me from their violet
And their furious atoms,

Its loving cover
Burns the junk of space
Over my watching eyes.

12

Thomas, you came from the sun.
We all did,
We were born from her body many years ago.

And now she nourishes us
And raises us up
In this her most thoughtfully made garden.

You will succeed me,
I am your sea-anchor,
My stomach is your terra-firma.

And when the sun's power
Of holding even herself in life should fade,
She will burst outwards in flame

Bringing our sleeping elements
To her same state again.

13

Carnation heart,
Heart of the flesh
And the bounded blood,
You still continue to bloom

In your shifting shades
Of afternoon blue
In rooms caressed by
Pale fingers of sky.

In greyest places you leap
And throw out paths of order,
Or pierce through surfaces
Causing light to glow in their depths.

Each shape that I destroy
You have considered for centuries
Without joy, without sorrow,
Without a face, without a mask.

Part 2
White Tulip

White Tulip

If I live a million years
I'll never meet a man who is what he thinks he is
And I myself
Will never be quite what I think I am.

Since this is so
Today I can walk in the park,
Things being all right all wrong,
And see human lovers on the grass
Mocked by this tulip's white perfection.

Solaris

after Stanislaw Lem

I was alone in the empty ocean;
Along came a spar of wood,
I clung to it

As it was dry,
For who knows how long.
It became, however, waterlogged

And sank, the ocean empty again
And I adrift. But look,
Along came a dry spar.

I took it, clung to it
For who knows how long,
Another lifetime, till it too

Took on water and went down
Into this empty and featureless sea,
But came another dry spar

And I started to understand
That this ocean itself did produce them
As this ocean did take them away,

And how should I explain this to
Those on the mainland
Drowning?

Vanishing

for Cathy Porter

There's a door half open
By a small cave where incense burns,
I stop in the dark

(Strange day in another country)

Orange light flares from the hearth
And I know this incense
Through years of sleep

A flame almost beyond desire
Burning against the immense
Perfectly still breastbone of space.

The staircase descends before us
While around the air sings 'mystery lives'
It's bread among stones, I take it.

Although it snows now so fast
We no longer leave prints,
There's still something to be gathered up
In this ecstasy and given

Although small houses
Sleep under snow
And ancestors lay flowers
As though we were already dead

There's still the difference
'Vive la différence'
Between us and them,
Between me and you
Between silence and the great cry from beyond silence
That folds into silence again and again

If only they knew! Between empty space
And two people holding hands under it
What a difference!

Small houses, dying lights,
You mark out a cross for your first-born
But the angel takes you all

And the great laws
And the great thoughts vanish,
The sad small houses
Vanish into the snow.

But coming back to my day in the country.
You, my love, you were so good –

Even without saying or thinking anything
We were *there*

Two creatures feeling awkward together
Because our own kind was vanishing

Out of such a universe,

With so little thought,
After so little time
Just vanishing.

Lullaby

for Rosie

That you live
May be a miracle;
That you came so late
May be a tragedy,
I don't want to say so,
Or say that the old sea
Won't yield for you her store
Of shells, living and dead
As she did for me
   Rock a bye baby

As you clutch at sweet air
Men clutch
The rifled butt of death
But you are so pleased with our welcome
Your smile when you wake
Would forgive even them
   Rock a bye baby

It's all for you now, miracle,
In this present that men fought for
And died for and were cut from the gibbet
Or firing post in the still morning
To forgive your tenderness a moment
That it might live
And flower a little
   Till the bough breaks.

Requiem

for Dennis Butt

1

I woke because it was morning
And because a child came in.

I woke, then, and found myself
A man looking at a child

Who had come in bearing her inheritance,
A child's freedom of morning.

I was aware I touched a common thing,
(man looking at child)

With a frightening thing, selfhood.
That I should be here, alive,
Looking at a child.

The dead don't see this.
Over us the flesh moves

Like moss upon stones.
We are the river.

2

Do we contradict the dead?
We living, they dead?

The dead looked at their children
And had eyes of life.

We look on our children
And will have eyes of death.

We and the dead look together
Through life, through death.

But why seeing
Here
Now?

Who?

3

After twenty four years I came back to your grave.
There were poems, music, an oration.
Four friends carried the box
To a wild place under a tree.

Unchanged the wild place, the tree.
I left, moved, moved again,
Grew up, moved, had children,
Moved again

Almost to that place where all that time
Your face and hands and feet
Had lain,
Your arms, your ribs, the heart which gave up on you
Were lying perfectly still.

And the clouds rolled over your grave
And for all you could hear
I was a cloud rolling over your grave.
I bent down to tell you
About all who had come after,
But you were right, they were clouds,
They were gone.

4

Even on a bright spring day
Sleet and rain appear.
The living come in from the cold.

But the dead, laid under trees,
Bare their chests to the rain.
Equally for the snow
And the fingers of frost
Their arms lie open in acceptance.

We, the living, have decided
That the dead shall bear the rain.

They go out without complaining
As though suddenly become brave.

5

In the vault light breaks.
In the vault rain collects.

The rain falls catching the light
Which frowns out of the clouds like the eye of God

Painting the child in the eye of the man.

Light echoes between the objects of the universe,
The ghost of matter, painting the unreachable.

All this light-painted world
Is not for the dead,
Are they any more wrong than we are?

Having lived and loved
They lie quietly under the flowers
Not disturbing us with non-existence,

Accepting not our memories
Nor the remnants of love

But the long cold rain
As light perpetual.

Inside the Whale

for Jonah Porter (20 July–22 August 1988)

1

You opened your eyes
Small fish flickered in the pool
And were lost again in the deep.

Little figure, struggling with your wooden lungs
Up the hill towards your Calvary
What messages reached you from our world?

Touch, music perhaps?
A shining light
Faces crowded round your cot you could not see.

Christ said all exists through the grace of God
Hui Neng said nothing exists
Heisenberg said everything almost certainly doesn't exist.

We live on a branch of baroque improbability
We are its smallest unfolding leaves
Given enough time and emptiness
No possible story that can't be written somewhere.

2

Did you dream inside the whale
Of what it is to be a man?

A Mozart, a Picasso, or a man
Driving in shirtsleeves through the night
To visit a sick baby in his cot?

Did you dream (even) of what it is to be loved,
To be belched up by the whale

To be beached on a warm breast
Between a pair of loving hands?

To be a man is to be twice shipwrecked
And left awake upon the sands.

3

Your face, when we saw it first in death
Seemed old and pinched and sad
As if to say
'Forgive me if I can't be beautiful,
Can't be the one you wanted after all'

My fear is that you knew you had to fight for love
And that to fight and win was all your strength.

You won,
But it was all you could do.

And then you picked your time
(Did you know she was there,
Your mother, outside the whale?)

Pricked in the hands and feet and side
You left us all you had for testament,
Your sad, grey face.

Forgive us, Jonah, as we forgive you
You were a warrior
You won everything except life
Which is a painful fit between two sleeps
That neither trouble us

But which is conscious in the depths.
Why else should the heart beat?
Why else the sad grey face?

4

And now it has been arranged.
There is an entry in the book,

For our last meeting.
And there is time now

To wander awhile
These leafy avenues.

No one has come with us.
But a black car
Picks its way among the graves

Bringing a coffin smaller than any I have ever seen,
Small and white like a starched sailor cap.

A single stranger is pallbearer
He places it before the fire

And we wait for the doors to open
For the plinth to move

And then I understand
That they are waiting.

The strangers
From the black car
Are waiting for us.

This is our moment of farewell.

Rosemary

for Maxine Northwood

It could be a woman
Or a girl child
Or even some small town in America

But in this,
'Rosemary is for remembrance'
It means simply a plant

That grows by your door.
Woody to the touch,
Pungent when crushed

As, indeed, is memory
Which gives, as the plant,
A perfumed bolt which strikes and grows.

It seems the nearest to enduring love
That I will ever know
Is that we two now, though careful not to touch

Still speak warmly to each other
And that seventeen years ago
We brought a boy-child home together after such

Traumas and searchings and sullenness.
Root stem and branch were we three then
And still there's joining somewhere deep below

We dare not talk about,
As though the woody stem had changed its name
From purest oak to sparest rosemary.

The Flower Arrangement

for EP Thompson, who went out to pick blackberries and died under his favourite magnolia bush

According to thought
If the mass of an electron
Were changed by one part in fifty million
There would be no space,
No stars,
No water,
No flesh,
No magnolia
And none of this need ever have happened.

So can we touch
The ground
Of so much possibility?
Or must we always dream
Away from the dark
As the price
Of being on loan
From the impossible?

For it is impossible, the dark,
We can never go into it.
We may go out in family groups to pick apples
Or strawberries, we can go gleaning in pairs
But only alone
Can the blackberry
Ever be tasted.

So are we mere flames
And is all this just shadows?

If it is, are there walls
The shadows play upon?
If so, what are they made of
And why can't we see them?
If not, how have we gone on
Fooling ourselves for so long?
And if we are just flames
Dancing in darkness
Does the walk to the magnolia tree take time
Or are we already there? Is it just
A dream in the dark that lets us say
'No, not us, not now,
Here are apples to pick,
There is time to walk in the grass
Together, there are birds
There are streams, there are flowers.'

Only one hand
Could have arranged this bouquet,
Set the black fruit against the green magnolia;
There was a flower arranger here,
Skillfully working,
Cutting and planting with never a mark
Save when someone misunderstood
A carefully laid out frame
Or picked up a scythe
That had gently been set down to rest.

And though many can gather the laurel
Or pluck the early blooming rose
Only the strong cut magnolia,
Only the strong grasp the blackberry by the root,
Turn Death about on his own doorstep
And say, 'There, you old fool, I mastered you,
I slipped your mask and showed your human face
And made of you a garland for the flames.'

Litakovo

*in memoriam Frank Thompson,
executed June 1944 at Litakovo, Bulgaria*

A bugle plays The Last Post, we lay flowers
And for a moment are as still as you.

Fifty years ago you gave your life
For something that I still can't find a name for,
Does it matter?
Only the deadened spirit needs to ask
Why one should give his whole life, everything,
The doing answers for itself. It seems
A monument is sealed
Wherever youth stands upon honour until death,
The touchstone of the real.

Here, no-one comes, no flowers fade,
Time gathers dust over a soldier's grave,
I stand within the shadows
Knowing you are close
And are as well as I am when I sleep
Knowing no more than you do when I'll wake.

After the Chinese

Seeing no sense in the world
I find an old hut to follow the steps of my teacher.
Even on a hot summer day
Yards of snow fly off the roof.

Four Brontë Pictures

1 *Wuthering Heights*

for Jonah Porter

When those tumultuous passions could no longer be contained
There were three mounds covered with moss
With all that beneath them as though it had never been

And the wind sailing over
As though nothing could ever disturb anything
In a place so green.

We scattered your ash on a day full of sun –
All these years on
Is there a single speck of your heart that has not been removed
      by the rain,

Yet isn't it, after all, we who depart
And you who remain?

2 *Agnes Grey*

Everything was true,
The spoilt children who wouldn't take no for an answer,

The drunken lords and prick-teasing ladies,
The cultivated grounds, the vistas

Of unwithered acres you could have unfolded
Your freedom across if anyone had given you the map.

Everything was true,
Sundays in church in the family pew

The handsome curate catching your eye,
The dream, the possibility –

Everything was true
Except the happy ending.

So we can look down our noses at you,
Anne, you missed the beanfeast.

If you could just have held out another century or so
You could have been like us –

Happy ending after
Happy ending after
Happy ending.

3 *Jane Eyre*

Five thousand apiece, that was a good notion –
That meant you all had money, forever,

And could afford to sit sometimes
On lazy sunlit lawns, listening

To the faint hum of engines
Powering towards you from over the century's rim.

4 Interior at Haworth

Here Death smiles at the living, it can wait
For the great feast which gathers at its gate
A culture gone into peripheries;

Outside the wind saps the trees, unaware
Of the spoiled century queuing at the door
Past gravestones slouching, blackened by the rain
As though exhausted by the world of form
And anxious to return from whence they came.

Inside I cannot find you. There are things
That once belonged to you:
Impossibly small, your visiting dress
Stalled, vacated, caged in glass;
Shoes, smaller than impossible,
Pebble lenses, fragments of script,
Three portraits, one flattering,
One bad, one painted from a memory,

They cannot touch your centre, but hold back
As though entirely shouldered off
By blazing whiteness burgeoning,
Filling centre frame.

His Master's Voice

for Jacob Porter

Walking in Piccadilly with my son
I see a familiar image of a gramophone
With a dog listening at the horn

And find my time has come round to explain
How strange all that once seemed,
Sound trapped on plates, the silent run

Of the thorn point in from the edge
To where mad dogs and Englishmen
Walked in the mid-day sun, Prokofiev's

Bird ascended in a flute
Stalked by clarinets in morning suits,
Where with each winding of the spring
Abdul Abulbul bit his scarf
And died for me, again, again, again.

It was such simple magic, anyone
Who'd felt the skin jump on a drum
Could understand how music, fed to wax,
Could live in album leaves like photographs,

The mystery was why it took so long
With hardly anything in the machine
That couldn't have been fashioned in the bronze
Age, or that of Brahms, Liszt, Schumann, Chopin.

It seems we inhabit islands lapped by time,
Each scarcely linked to each, though your delight
As the hi-fi belts out disco hits just might
Be a passing wave to mine at the horn's rim.

Before the Flood

for EP Thompson

1

These lines and knots of silver lace
Mark where light passed by a tree

And that a tree stood in such a place
Is proved by them. And whether by luck

Or skill, it came out a good shot,
The boyish face is clear of shadow, concentrates

On the ripe fruit beneath the hands
While Autumn waits.

Many times I saw him, as a man
Pick fruit from a tree, knowing nothing

Of the boy standing in this calm
Before the flood-tide broke.

2

How can a summer meadow seem
More spacious clipped at two by two
Than any I have ever seen?

Perhaps the light, before the flood,
Knew how to paint a denser shade of white,

Perhaps the Word
Was at large
And the bromide echoed it,

Or perhaps the cause is a smallish boy
In knee length shorts and a floppy hat

Extending his negligent, easy limbs
On the back of a five barred gate

As though he had just read Huckleberry Finn
And was cruising the rivers in state

Without even a hint of the murmuring flood
Soon to break over that tousled head
As the rivers swapped water for blood.

3

Three boys by a rock face making for a climb.

Bleached and pixellated this one. I take a glass
To it, and yes,

I can make out my father's, high cheek bones,
His eyes already lamp-sharp, before they'd known
All they learned he'd never talk about.

I picture them at day's end, pleasantly worn,
Toweling boy's sweat, every hand and foothold,
Every minor slip lived over again
In the vicarious safety of the den.

Unconscious of the cliffs they'd have to face,
Of the slipped grasp, the shattered rose.

4

An older boy in army kit
Looks down at a dog. It's bad light,

His smile gawks – I can't tell from here
Whether through embarrassment or fear,

Janus like. The backdrop's white
As though the flood had bleached it out of sight

And I can almost hear the bleached farewells
The edges of this frame incarcerate.

5

Of this family group in Xmas '31
No-one now remains.
The elder of the boys died,
Exhausted, forthright, resigned
By an executioner's gun.

Waiting, not knowing if he was alive or dead
The father withered in angst.
The mother did survive,
Though not the youthful smile
She wears on this negative.

Of this family group in '31
None now remain.
Trailing your foot in the sand
You outlived them all, taking a long walk
On the short beach of these recollections.

Now you have joined them in that place
Where no-one tastes their memories

But offers them as fading images
To become, for this instant, ours.

6

I come back to the tree.
You have not moved,
But stand in dappled shadow as before,
Caught in that pose as though eternity
Held you against the light for a better view.

Any year of our life
I could have seen you with a basket in your hands
Climb for ivy, strip an apple bough –

Many times we picked together
And always in silence. Now I see

That we were not so distant in our age ,
It was the flood that stopped me reaching out

To the boy in these old pictures
And the silence was his shout.

The Bells

From Tübingen to Kloster Bebenhausen you hear them,
Crazy Zildjians, hammering spun gold solitons around their
       shocked rims.

Bong
     Bong
          Bong, their flaws
Screech at the fifth or roar at the octave's crack
If you've ears for that unholy circus
Of dim demons riding the angel's back.

Their tones chase each other like cubs on a riverbank,
Join hands in a ring and dance a ring a ring a roses,
Spew out pale ghosts like the drowned bells at Dunwich,
Howl with pain as though each contained Popeye's fist
              and a whole tin of spinach,

Hurl at us the primal mystery
Which is that sleeping bronze
Withholds such a song.

Or else they catch you in the Markt Platz,
Raining sound upon you and they
Pound,
     Pound,
          Pound. Your one defense
Is to abandon all defenses and go stumm
As the sound floods into you like pain
Slowly turning to joy, breaks into you,
Splatters your walls with gold, calls to you
To wake if you still can, to be clear
Once more, taut and resonant
As a bronze throat subtending air...

Against the parade
Of tinny hi-fi
And burgherly insomnia
Long may they stand.

Waves on Water

1

In Coole Park at the lake's edge
A sheltering stone I've sometimes sat below
To watch the wind throw shards upon the lough
A mirror laid, shattered, made anew

A flash of grief that on this sacred block
Children have scratched names, that such was here
And so and so loves such and such tears
And frees the heart, in an instant's shear

Of comprehension and relief
That names are empty as the wind
And traced in ink or scratched in stone
Natural as waves on water and as brief.

2

Consider your life as a sealed room;
Behind, the entrance you can neither stoop nor see,
Ahead the dull exit door
Stone, steel and wishing cannot bar
Yet never opens though it glows and cools.

Finally the bolt slips back,
Your startled eyes follow the bright chink
Up to the lintel expecting a tall figure in black

Whilst in under your gaze slips a laughing and dancing child.

3

How did you come to be there?
After so long walking on a forest path
You turned a bend and came upon a gate
In a mild clearing filled with summer air

You knew only that this was the end of roads
A terminus not on any map
And not described by any history
This space of pure negation into which light crowds,

At once empty and populated still
By all who passed before
Your father, waiting, took your hand
You bathed in strangeness as a waterfall.

Not in Your Name

When the *Wehrmacht* went into Poland
You were packed off to crawl in earth,
Were butchered in batches
Rubber-stamped with date and time of death,

Were changed by History's rolling mill
From raw boys with aching balls
To pressed flowers in pressed fatigues
Gazing, unrequited still
Into the backs of album leaves.

It is to your memory that I offer my shame

That our country now,
Not to defend Liberty
But to avenge Money
Destroys poor folk who cannot save themselves.

But not in your name!

Soldiers

*Go tell the Spartans, passer-by,
That here, obedient to their wish we lie.*
          Simonides (Thermopylae)

I come to protest the deaths of soldiers
    huddled in barracks, sweating in trenches
dragged from their farms, their factories
    a gun, a gas mask and a mess can
a khaki coat you are no longer a man
    you are a goalpost, a snooker pocket
a bullet through your brain
    just deuce, a match point, a black potted
when exactly did you lose the right to live,
    when your call-up papers landed on the mat?
or when they were put in the post?
    when your name was written into the lists?
or when the midwife hauled you from the howling womb
    looked between your legs and pronounced you man,
        guilty as charged?

I will not waste time protesting the deaths of children
    which is an industry, whole factories, industrial estates
already thrive on, every day whole forests are felled
    whole oceans of synthetic tears are wept dry for them
their cute, muddy or preferably bloodstained faces
    are stacked in libraries back to back like celluloid corpses,
are whisked off optical-magnetic media, telegraphed at the
        speed of light
every editor is hungry for more and each has their favourite
    and I will not waste time protesting the deaths of women who
        are all innocent

even though year after year they go to the polls
    and vote first, second and third preference for Death, Death, Death
yet they miraculously remain innocent,
    yes, it seems that no matter how much power they have
to vote, to choose, no matter how punctually their demands must be fulfilled
their innocence astonishingly expands to cover all
    like a pink blanket, soft and warm
exhaling a faint whiff of TV dinners and contraceptive foam

guilt lands on the shoulders of the soldier
    a khaki doll, wind him up and he'll crawl through hell
tick tock, regular as a clock
    you, the customer, can choose, mean look one or fierce look two,
did you ever see a frightened soldier doll?
    guilt lands as white hot uranium splattered into his tank
as cluster bombs blowing off feet and arms
    ten thousand country boys blown to one column inch at Kandahar
fear, pain and shit in his pants
    is that your finger on the trigger, brother, or mine?
is that your guilt on my shoulders, brother, or mine?
    and your name? Oh really? I also am Unknown.

today I want you to forget about innocence,
    about women, children and other icons
whose deaths will still be there tomorrow to comfort you
    who will keep you safely indignant for years to come
and spend just one day thinking about soldiers.
    thank them for their age-old courtesy, their habit
of not cluttering up your newspapers with their complaints
    of not ringing your private telephones off the wall

but just quietly shuffling up the line
    collecting a gun, a gas mask and a mess can
iron rations and an honorary doctorate in dying
    and reflect
that though there are, indeed, enemies
    there are no enemy soldiers,
so that the guilt may finally be lifted
    and their crushed souls rest in peace.

    in peace.

Joanna

There were yellow flowers on the mountain
And peach blossom, speckled pink
Presided over by the lofty trunks
Of a few arboreal antiques

You, beautiful when angry
Are always angry, therefore
Always beautiful, you sat

On the top of a wall like a cat
With your little red shoes
Pulled tight against your hips,
Toes towards me

As if to say, 'look,
My feet are still bound.'

As for Forever

for Dorothy Thompson

1

The infant heart
Leaves the hand of darkness
Like a boomerang slipped from the hand of a hunter
Flailing and turning
Upwards and outwards
Thrashing the fleeing blood
Gathering its harvest of light

Gradually turned
By tiny imperfections mounting air
Into a returning arc,
Its last and bravest beat
A sharp slap
Into the hunter's waiting hand.

2

Your things come back from the ward
Packed neatly, as ever

A pair of slippers, reading specs,
A purse with loose change,

A sponge bag,
A thriller, hardly begun

Plot suspended,
Characters waiting,

Patiently bookmarked,
To be opened again in the next world.

3

Death is not the end
But the farthest wall
Of the hall that houses us.
As for forever,
We can only imagine it.

Without birth there is no death
Without death, no birth;
As the newborn know nothing
So the dead regain all innocence.

The living give birth to the newborn
And the living give death to the dying;
Birth is dangerous
For mother and child,
So also is death,
For the dying and those gathered at the bier

For all must be given and forgiven
In that last, strange, courageous beat,
As the heart completes its arc.

4

I return to the house where you lived,
Strange, now, these streets
That no longer lead to you

But, purged by the departure of great spirits
Gleam now, blackly
As though freshly swept by rain.

To sit now, watching these things
Transform themselves from being yours
To being mere discards of the dead

Quietly shedding your memory, to become
Boot-sale bric-a-brac,
The flotsam of time.

3

Death is not the end
But the farthest wall
Of the hall that houses us.
As for forever,
We can only imagine it.

Without birth there is no death
Without death, no birth;
As the newborn know nothing
So the dead regain all innocence.

The living give birth to the newborn
And the living give death to the dying;
Birth is dangerous
For mother and child,
So also is death,
For the dying and those gathered at the bier

For all must be given and forgiven
In that last, strange, courageous beat,
As the heart completes its arc.

4

I return to the house where you lived,
Strange, now, these streets
That no longer lead to you

But, purged by the departure of great spirits
Gleam now, blackly
As though freshly swept by rain.

To sit now, watching these things
Transform themselves from being yours
To being mere discards of the dead

Quietly shedding your memory, to become
Boot-sale bric-a-brac,
The flotsam of time.

5

You died in your sleep, they say,
Meaning in the depths of night

Although I know you did not sleep
And that that last beat of your heart
Was a gift for us,

A final word,
A fist enclosing flowers.

Tables

My mother gave me a table
And told me to take special care
As though time itself would have an end
When tables must be accounted for

To an old maker in a dusty shirt
Who'd carefully rub out each stain
Peering reproachfully through rimless specs
When he came to the spot where the lamp flamed

Till finally it would be as new,
As bright and clear as polished glass
While outside, lovers long since dead
Walked arm in arm in the summer grass.

Acknowledgements

Some of these poems go back forty years and more. 'Four Brontë Pictures' was first published in *The Interpreter's House*; 'His Master's Voice' was first published in *The Spokesman*, 'Requiem' and 'Vanishing' were first published with a Chinese translation by Li Wan (李琬) in Fei Di (飞地).